MOUNTAIN

Sean Callery

Consultant: David Burnie

KINGFISHER

NEW YORK

KINGFISHER
LONDON & NEW YORK

Copyright © Kingfisher 2012
Published in the United States by Kingfisher,
175 Fifth Ave., New York, NY 10010
Kingfisher is an imprint of Macmillan Children's Books, London.
All rights reserved.

Distributed in the U.S. and Canada by Macmillan,
175 Fifth Ave., New York, NY 10010

Library of Congress Cataloging-in-Publication data has been applied for.

ISBN: 978-0-7534-6810-4

Kingfisher books are available for special promotions and premiums.
For details contact: Special Markets Department, Macmillan,
175 Fifth Ave., New York, NY 10010.

For more information, please visit www.kingfisherbooks.com

Printed in China
1 3 5 7 9 8 6 4 2
1TR/0312/UTD/WKT/140MA

Note to readers: the website addresses listed in this book are correct at
the time of going to print. However, due to the ever-changing nature
of the Internet, website addresses and content can change. Websites
can contain links that are unsuitable for children. The publisher cannot
be held responsible for changes in website addresses or content or for
information obtained through a third party. We strongly advise that
Internet searches be supervised by an adult.

The publisher would like to thank the following for permission to reproduce their material. Every care has been taken to trace copyright holders. However, if there
have been unintentional omissions or failure to trace copyright holders, we apologize and will, if informed, endeavor to make corrections in any future edition.

Top = t; Bottom = b; Center = c; Left = l; Right = r

All artwork Stuart Jackson-Carter (Peter Kavanagh Art Agency)

Cover main Shutterstock/Walter G. Arce; covertl Getty/Animals Animals; covertcl Getty/All Canada Photos; covtcr FLPA/Donald Jones/Minden; covertr Shutterstock/mlorenz; bk
covertr Naturepl/Stephen Dalton; bk covercl Shutterstock/Arkady; bk covercr Shutterstock/Perrush; bk coverbl Shutterstock/Steve Collendar; and pages 1 Shutterstock/Takahashi
Photography; 2 Shutterstock/Rafa Irusta; 3t Shutterstock/MonicaOttino; 3b Shutterstock/Matyas Arval; 4t Shutterstock/seawhisper; 4b Shutterstock/Serg Zastavkin; 5t Shutterstock/
svehlik; 5b Shutterstock/Dirk Brink; 6l Naturepl/Andy Sands; 6tr Naturepl/Kim Taylor; 6br Getty/OSF; 7tl Alamy/blickwinkel/Hecker; 7tr Shutterstock/Sari ONeal; 7ct Shutterstock/
Artistas; 7c Shutterstock/Cre8tive Images; 7cb Getty/RHPL; 7bl FLPA/Fabio Pupin; 7r Shutterstock/Kuttelvaserova; 7br Shutterstock/Maksimilian; 7bc Shutterstock/felizy; 8l
Photoshot/NHPA/Bill Coster; 8tr Naturepl/Markus Varesvuo; 8br Alamy/Rick & Nora Bowers; 9tl Getty/Muehlmann K; 9tr Shutterstock/Pefkos; 9ct Shutterstock/Vadim Davydov; 9c
Shutterstock/Vadim Davydov; 9cb Shutterstock/Maksimilian; 9bl Getty/OSF; 9r Shutterstock/Roberto Cerruti; 9br Shutterstock/Redwood; 9bc Shutterstock/Linda Macpherson; 10l
Photoshot/NHPA/Robert Erwin; 10tr Naturepl/Stephen Dalton; 11tl Getty/Animals Animals; 11tr Shutterstock/Steve Collendar; 11ct Naturepl/Stephen Dalton; 11c Naturepl/Stephen
Dalton; 11cb Shutterstock/Redwood; 11bl repl/Stephen Dalton; 11r Shutterstock/Bruce MacQueen; 11br Shutterstock/Stayer; 11bc Shutterstock/vilax; 12l Ardea/M. Watson; 12tr
Getty/First Light Associated Photographers; 12br Corbis/Daniel J. Cox; 13tl FLPA/Sergey Korschkov; 13tr Shutterstock/Steve Byland; 13ct Getty/OSF; 13c Shutterstock/Meolta; 13cb
Alamy/tbkmedia.de; 13bl Photoshot/NHPA/Eero Murtomaki; 13r Shutterstock/Steve Byland; 13br Shutterstock/Meolta; 13bc Shutterstock/Martha Marks; 14l FLPA/Luciano
Candisani; 14tr FLPA/Michael Krabs/Imagebroker; 14br Shutterstock/Vadim Koziovsky; 15tl Alamy/Eric Gevaert; 15tr Shutterstock/Lee319; 15ct Shutterstock/Steshkin Yevgeniy; 15c
Shutterstock/Steshkin Yevgeniy; 15cb Shutterstock/Steshkin Yevgeniy; 15bl Naturepl/Steimer/ARCO; 15cr Shutterstock/Dr. Morley Read; 15br Getty/OSF; 15b Shutterstock/Dr.
Morley Read; 16l FLPA/Claus Meyer/Minden; 16tr Getty/OSF; 17tl Naturepl/Hanne & Jens Eriksen; 17tr stock/Dr. Morley Read; 17ct FLPA/Claus Meyer/Minden; 17cb Getty/Peter
Arnold; 17br Shutterstock/Walter G. Arce; 18l Getty/Peter Arnold; 18tr Getty/Animals Animals; 18br Getty/All Canada Photos; 19tl Shutterstock/mlorenz; 19tr Shutterstock/Steve
Hermann; 19ct Shutterstock/Daniel Hebert; 19c Shutterstock/Arie v.d. Wolde; 19cb Shutterstock/Jill Lang; 19bl FLPA/Donald Jones/Minden; 19cr Shutterstock/Arkady; 19br
Shutterstock/mlorenz; 19b Shutterstock/Snowbelle; 20l SPL/Nature's Images; 20tr SPL/CDC, J. Gathany; 20br Alamy/Dylan Becksholt; 21tl FLPA/Mark Moffett/Minden; 21tr
Shutterstock/Mary Terriberry; 21ct SPL/CDC; 21c SPL/Susumu Nishinaga; 21cb SPL/CDC; 21bl Alamy/Dylan Becksholt; 21cr Shutterstock/Robert Biedermann; 21br Getty/
Cuboimages; 21b Shutterstock/Ljjuan Guo; 22l FLPA/Reinhard Holzl/Imagebroker ; 22tr Getty/Cuboimages; 23tr Shutterstock/Falk Klenas; 23ct SPL/Claude Nurisany & Marie
Perennou; 23c Alamy/Maximilian Weinzierl; 23cb FLPA/Bob Gibbons; 23cr Shutterstock/Falk Klenas; 23br Shutterstock/Vladimir Mucibabic; 24l Shutterstock/bcampbell65; 25tl
Naturepl/Eric Dragesco; 25tr Shutterstock/Doug Lemke; 25ct Shutterstock/Vladimir Mucibabic; 25c Shutterstock/Igor Mikjakin; 25cb Shutterstock/Ssnowball; 25bl Alamy/Michal
Cerny; 25cr Shutterstock/Doug Lemke; 25br Shutterstock/worldswildlife wonders; 25b Shutterstock/Tamara Kulikova; 26l FLPA/Paul Sawer; 26tr FLPA/Terry Whittaker; 26br Alamy/
Terry Whittaker; 27tl Corbis/Verge; 27c Shutterstock/Ervin Monn; 27tr Shutterstock/tomas bonnefoy1; 27ct Shutterstock/Stayer; 27c Shutterstock/BMCL; 27cb Corbis/Alan Carey;
27tl FLPA/Cyril Ruoso/Minden; 27cr Shutterstock/linerpics; 27br Shutterstock/Karen Kane; 27b Shutterstock/Robert Biedermann; 30tl Shutterstock/Perrush; 30b Shutterstock/Sari
ONeal; 31tr Shutterstock/Marian Wilson; 31bc Shutterstock/Maxim Pushkarev; 31br Shutterstock/Doug Lemke; 32tl Shutterstock/Hway Klong Lim; 32tr Shutterstock/Michael
Woodruff; 32br Shutterstock/Fremme

Contents

Introduction

Mountains are cold, high, and rocky, so plants and animals must be tough to survive. Birds may fly elsewhere, but most other animals stay near shelter and food.

Every living thing needs food in order to survive. With few plants in the mountains, many animals survive by eating each other. The list of who eats whom is called a food chain.

Next in the chain are animals that survive by eating plants. They are known as consumers. The red squirrel is one, eating seeds, nuts, and berries.

Food chain 1
Rocky Mountains

NORTH AMERICA

Equator

Food chain 3
Andes Mountains

SOUTH AMERICA

At the bottom of a food chain are the producers: plants that make their own food using the sun's energy. The white dryas is one of these. It lives in Europe and North America.

Bigger, faster animals prey on the plant eaters. Some plants also trap and digest insects. The beech marten eats mice and squirrels, as well as insects and fruit. It lives in Europe and Central Asia.

This book takes you along three food chains from mountains in different parts of the world. You will learn about the life cycles of ten animals and one plant: how they are born, grow, reproduce, and die.

EUROPE

ASIA

AFRICA

Food chain 2
Himalayas

AUSTRALIA

At the top of a food chain is an animal that is too fast, big, or strong to be attacked. The Cape eagle owl from southern Africa hunts mammals even if they are heavier than itself.

Earwig

Earwigs hide in damp places, such as soil and rotting trees in the Rocky Mountains. They come out at night to eat plants and to scavenge dead insects.

1 The female lays about 50 eggs in a hole in the ground. She turns them to keep them clean. The eggs absorb water and could get moldy if she failed to do this.

2 After about a month, the female spreads the eggs out and they hatch into tiny earwigs, called nymphs.

4 After a month, the growing nymphs shed their outer skin and leave the nest. Adult earwigs shelter under the soil during the winter and come out to feed and mate in the spring.

3 She stays with her young, bringing food for them and fighting off predators. This behavior is very unusual among insects.

Did you know?

Earwigs have a pair of pincers that they use to defend themselves and to help fold away their wings.

They have biting mouthparts to chew up plants and insects, both dead and alive. They also use their mouths to clean their bodies.

Earwigs have an outer layer called an exoskeleton to stop their bodies from drying out and to protect them from attack.

Earwigs live for about 2 years. They hide away in holes, but some predators are very good at tugging them out . . .

Woodpecker

The American three-toed woodpecker drills holes in tree trunks, hammering with its beak 16 times per second. That's almost 1,000 blows per minute! Inside the holes are insects and larvae that it licks up with its long, sticky tongue.

1 A pair of birds digs a nest in a dead tree each year. It can take them a month to make a big enough hole. Then they line the nest with chips of wood.

2 The female lays 3—4 white eggs. The color helps the parents see them in the dark. Both birds take turns to keep the eggs warm.

4 After a month, the chicks can fly. Soon they leave the nest for good. Woodpeckers like to hunt in dead trees killed by fire or flood, as these have the most insects.

3 The chicks hatch in about 2 weeks. Their parents feed them a mixture of insects and larvae, fruit, and tree sap.

Did you know?

A woodpecker's beak has strong bones at its center. Its nostrils are small to keep out chips of wood.

Stiff tail feathers help the bird hold steady while it hammers its beak into the tree trunk.

Strong neck muscles help absorb the shock of the hammering.

Woodpeckers may live for 6–8 years. Adults and their eggs are always at risk from predators, some from the air . . .

Flying squirrel

Northern flying squirrels do not really fly: they glide between trees and land on the ground to search for mushrooms, nuts, and fruit. They will also eat small birds and their eggs.

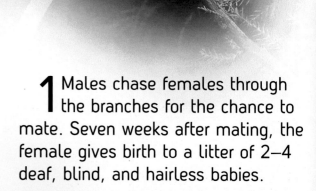

1 Males chase females through the branches for the chance to mate. Seven weeks after mating, the female gives birth to a litter of 2–4 deaf, blind, and hairless babies.

2 After a month, the babies' ears stand up and their eyes open. They have fur and grow to four times their birth weight by suckling their mother's rich milk.

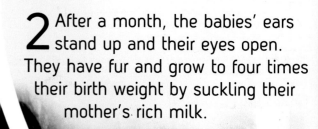

Did you know?

The "wings" are made of skin stretched between the body and the legs. They fold out of the way when the squirrel runs or climbs.

The tail is flat and helps the squirrel fly through the air and balance when it lands.

Squirrels have four front teeth that never stop growing. They wear down as the animals chew their food.

4 These squirrels are very sociable. A group often shares a tree nest. They huddle together to stay warm through the harsh winter, but they do not hibernate.

3 At 3 months old, they learn to glide. Within weeks, they will be able to take care of themselves.

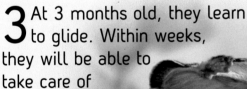

These squirrels live for about 4 years. Owls hunt them in the sky, but other predators sneak up on the ground . . .

11

Wolverine

A wolverine is the size of a dog, but it is fierce enough to fight and eat animals much larger than itself. It eats birds' eggs, squirrels, and even moose.

1 About every 2 years, the female builds a snow den high in the mountains. There, she gives birth to 2–3 babies, called kits. They are blind and have no teeth.

2 The mother nurses the kits for 3 months. She moves dens to stay away from attackers—the kits are in more danger now than at any other time in their lives.

12

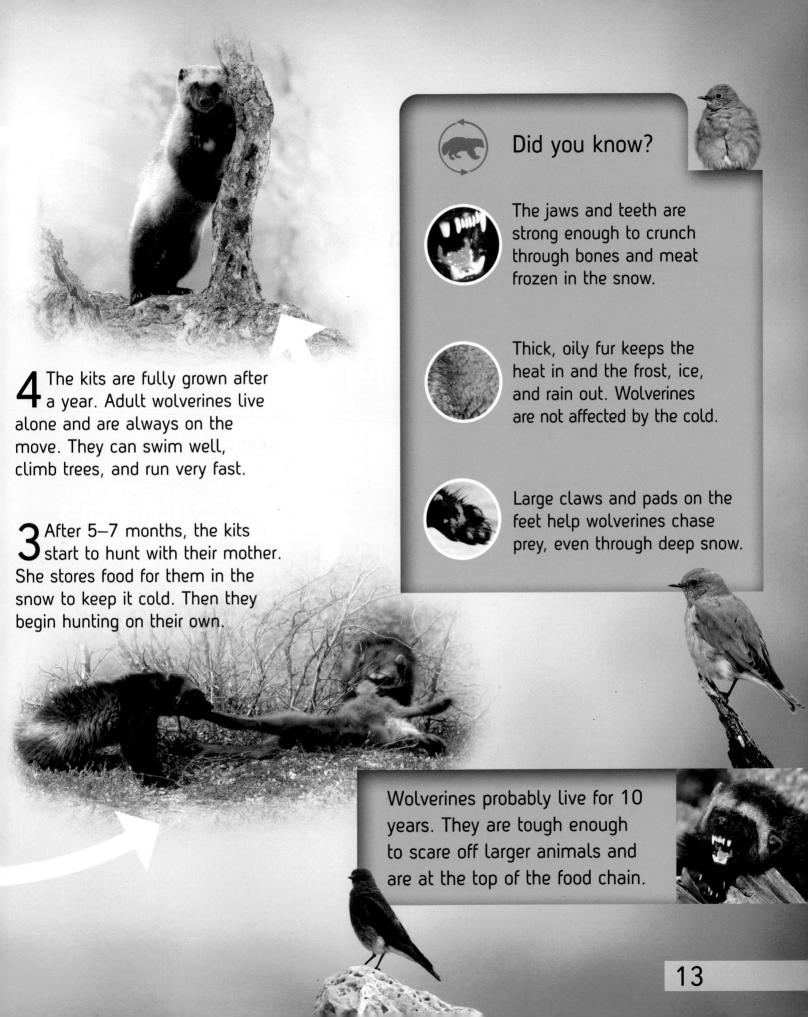

4 The kits are fully grown after a year. Adult wolverines live alone and are always on the move. They can swim well, climb trees, and run very fast.

3 After 5–7 months, the kits start to hunt with their mother. She stores food for them in the snow to keep it cold. Then they begin hunting on their own.

Did you know?

The jaws and teeth are strong enough to crunch through bones and meat frozen in the snow.

Thick, oily fur keeps the heat in and the frost, ice, and rain out. Wolverines are not affected by the cold.

Large claws and pads on the feet help wolverines chase prey, even through deep snow.

Wolverines probably live for 10 years. They are tough enough to scare off larger animals and are at the top of the food chain.

Mosquito

The Asian tiger mosquito feeds on plant sap and sweet nectar in the Himalayas. The females need more nutrients to make eggs, so they drink the blood of mammals and birds, too.

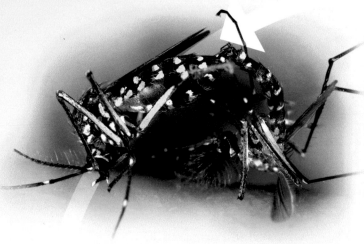

1 After mating, the female lays more than 200 black, oval eggs above the water. They hatch when the water level rises.

2 The eggs hatch into larvae that feed and swim using brushes in their mouths. They stay near the water's surface and breathe through tubes near their tails.

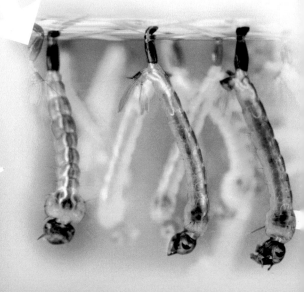

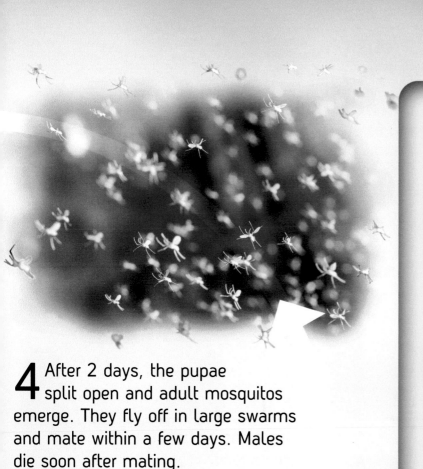

Did you know?

Mosquitos have a feeding tube called a proboscis. The female's is sharp so that it can pierce skin and take blood.

Mosquitos have a pair of long feelers on their heads called antennae, which sense smells and vibrations.

A female mosquito's body looks red when it has had a meal of blood.

4 After 2 days, the pupae split open and adult mosquitos emerge. They fly off in large swarms and mate within a few days. Males die soon after mating.

3 Over 5–10 days, the larvae grow in four stages and turn into pupae. They stop feeding, but still come up to the water's surface to breathe air.

Mosquitos only live for a few weeks and have many predators, one of which traps them in its sticky glue . . .

Alpine butterwort

Like most plants, the alpine butterwort makes its own food using sunlight, but it also traps insects, such as mosquitos, on its sticky leaves and slowly digests them.

1 In the spring, the plant opens its buds and leaves. The leaves are covered in a sticky liquid like glue that grips hold of any insects that land on them.

2 In the summer, the plant produces 6–8 flowers. Flies and bees visit the flowers to drink nectar. They pollinate the flowers at the same time.

4 The plant shrinks to a small rosette of leaves in the winter. Its seeds will germinate into new plants if they land on wet ground.

3 The plant develops seed capsules that hold many tiny, brown seeds. The light seeds are carried away by strong winds. They can travel several miles.

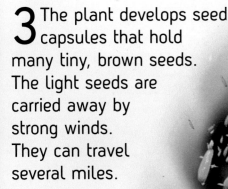

Did you know?

The edges of the sticky leaves often curl up to form cup shapes to hold and digest more prey.

Insects are guided to the nectar by the bright yellow patches on the flowers. They take pollen away when they leave and fertilize other plants.

The alpine butterwort has long roots that hold it in place in rocky and wet habitats.

The butterwort's sticky leaves trap insects for its food, but they cannot protect it from being eaten by larger animals . . .

Mountain goat

Mountain goats are skillful climbers. They jump and run on steep mountain slopes and cliffs, munching leaves, grass, herbs, and moss and staying away from predators.

1 Male goats fight to see who is the strongest and will mate with a female. They stand on their back legs and hit each other with their horns. This is called rutting.

2 About 6 months after mating, the female gives birth to one or sometimes two babies, known as kids.

18

4 Adult goats live in male or female herds of 10–20 animals. The different sexes only meet up once a year when it is time to mate.

3 The kids suckle milk from their mother for 6 months. It is very rich and full of nutrients, so the babies grow fast. Over time, they start to eat plants.

Did you know?

Mountain goats have excellent senses of sight, hearing, and smell and are always on the alert for danger.

If they cannot run away from a predator, they threaten it with their large, curved horns.

Each hoof is split into two toes. This makes the foot very flexible, so the goat can balance on uneven surfaces.

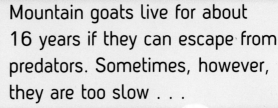

Mountain goats live for about 16 years if they can escape from predators. Sometimes, however, they are too slow . . .

Snow leopard

Snow leopards are sometimes called "ghost cats." They are quiet and almost invisible against the gray rock until they spring to seize the goats and sheep that are their prey.

1 Snow leopards mate every 2 years. About 100 days after mating, the female gives birth to a litter of 2–3 cubs in a rocky den lined with fur from her body.

2 The cubs are blind and helpless, but they already have a thick coat of black-spotted fur to keep them warm. Their eyes open after a week.

4 Young snow leopards travel long distances to find their own territories. As adults, they live alone. They kill their prey with a bite to the neck, then drag it to a safe place for eating.

3 The cubs can walk after a month. They start to leave the den after 3 months, but stay near their mother until they are about 2 years old.

Did you know?

Long, strong back legs give these cats the power to leap six times their body length.

Large, wide paws act like snowshoes to grip the slippery rock and ice of the mountains.

A thick, furry tail helps the leopard balance and can also be wrapped around the body like a warm scarf.

Snow leopards can live for about 15 years. No other animal is big, fierce, or fast enough to kill an adult leopard.

Chinchilla

Chinchillas are small rodents that live among the rocks high up in the Andes Mountains. They sleep in burrows during the day and come out at night to eat grass, seeds, and fruit.

1 Chinchillas mate for life. The mating season lasts from May to November, during which the female may have two litters.

2 About 4 months after mating, the female gives birth to 2–3 babies, called kits. They are well-developed with fur and teeth, and they can open their eyes at birth.

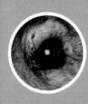

Large eyes help them see in the dark. They are most active at dusk and dawn, when there are fewer predators around.

4 Chinchillas are adult at 8 months old. They live in groups of about 50 animals, called herds. They clean each other and "talk" in chirps, squeaks, and barks.

Chinchilla fur is soft, silky, and keeps the animal warm in the cold of the high mountains.

Large ears help them survive the summer heat. Their blood is cooled as it flows through veins in their ears.

3 The kits suckle their mother's milk for 6—8 weeks before being weaned. They call out for food with high-pitched chirps.

Chinchillas can live for 10 years, but they make a tasty meal for a lot of animals . . .

Skunk

The Andes skunk will eat anything, from plants and berries to small mammals, such as chinchillas. It protects itself from its predators by spraying them with stinky liquid.

1 Skunks only come together to mate. In the early spring, the female digs a burrow, where she will give birth to her babies.

2 Two months after mating, a litter of 2–5 kits is born. They are blind, deaf, and covered in soft fur.

4 Skunks are fully grown at 7 months and leave the burrow 5 months later. They live alone, although females huddle together for warmth in the winter.

3 The kits can squirt their smelly scent at 3 weeks old, even before they are able to open their eyes. They suckle their mother's milk for 2 months.

Did you know?

Skunks have long, powerful front claws that they use for digging insects out of their nests and making burrows.

They have very good senses of smell and hearing but cannot see clearly farther than 10 feet (3 meters).

A skunk lifts its tail as a warning to attackers. If that fails, it sprays them with stinky liquid.

Skunks can live for 6 years, but some predators are not put off by their terrible smell . . .

Owl

The great horned owl can grab and carry off animals heavier than itself. It is a stalker that sees and hears everything and then swoops down on prey such as rabbits and skunks.

1 Once a year, the female lays 2–3 eggs in a nest taken over from another bird. She keeps them warm for 5 weeks, while she is fed and guarded by her mate.

2 Then the eggs hatch. The chicks demand food from their parents with loud hissing and screeching sounds.

4 A young owl may have several territories until it settles down and mates. It always hunts alone.

3 At 6 weeks old, the young owls hop onto nearby branches to practice balancing and perching. They begin to fly a week later. Both parents continue to feed them.

Did you know?

This owl gets its name from the large tufts on its head. They look like ears, but are simply feathers.

Owls have special, fluffy feathers on their wings that help them fly silently and take their prey by surprise.

Owls have four powerful, sharp talons on each foot, used for killing and carrying their prey.

Few predators threaten this owl once it is an adult, so it is at the top of its food chain. It can live for 10–13 years.

A Rocky Mountain food web

This book follows three mountain food chains.
Most animals eat more than one food, so they
are part of many food chains. There are a lot
of food chains in mountain habitats, and they
link up like a map to make a food web.

wolverine

flying squirrel

woodpecker

mountain lion,
or cougar or
puma

moose

spruce beetle

fungi

fruit

earwig

leaves

raccoon

Sun

Glossary

BURROW
A hole or tunnel in the ground, where an animal lives.

CONSUMER
A living thing that survives by eating other living things.

DEN
A wild animal's home.

DIGEST
When the body breaks food down to get nutrients.

EXOSKELETON
The hard layer on the outside of an insect's body.

FERTILIZE
When male and female sex cells join to form a new life.

GERMINATE
When a seed starts to grow.

HABITAT
The natural home of an animal.

HIBERNATE
When an animal rests through the winter.

LARVA
A young insect that will change its body shape to become an adult. Groups are called larvae.

LITTER
A group of baby animals born to the same mother at the same time.

MAMMAL
An animal that has fur and feeds milk to its babies.

MATE
When a male and female animal reproduce. For some animals, there is a particular time each year when they mate and this is called the "mating season."

NECTAR
The sweet liquid made by flowers to attract insects.

NUTRIENTS
Anything that a living thing takes in to give it energy and to help it grow.

NYMPH
A young insect that is not yet fully grown and has no wings.

PINCERS
A pair of grippers used to hold things.

POLLEN
A fine powder made by flowers that plants use in order to reproduce.

POLLINATE
To carry pollen from one flower to another, helping it reproduce.

PREDATOR
An animal that kills and eats other animals.

PREY
An animal hunted by a predator.

PRODUCER
A living thing, such as a plant, that makes its own food using the energy of the sun.

PUPA
The stage when a young insect rests while changing its body shape. Groups are called pupae.

RODENT
A gnawing animal, such as a rat or a mouse.

SAP
The liquid that flows inside a plant.

SCAVENGE
To search for and eat dead animals.

SEED CAPSULE
A container for seeds.

SUCKLE
When a baby mammal drinks milk from its mother.

SWARM
A large group of flying insects.

TERRITORY
An area of land where one animal or group of animals lives and hunts.

WEAN
When a baby stops drinking milk from its mother and eats solid food instead.

These websites have information about mountains or their animals—or both!

- enchantedlearning.com/biomes
- http://animals.nationalgeographic.com/animals/
- kidsplanet.org/factsheets/map.html
- vtaide.com/png/foodchains.htm
- wwf.panda.org/about_our_earth/ecoregions/about/habitat_types/habitats/mountains/

Index